The "Reason Why" Books

TASTE, TOUCH
AND
SMELL

Irving and Ruth Adler

612
Ad

The John Day Company   New York

The "Reason Why" Books
by Irving and Ruth Adler

Library of Congress Catalogue Card Number: 66-11448
PRINTED IN THE UNITED STATES OF AMERICA

Contents

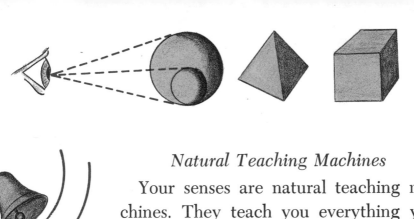

Natural Teaching Machines

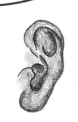

Your senses are natural teaching machines. They teach you everything you know about the world around you. They help you *perceive* (pur-SEEVE).

You perceive shapes, sizes, distances and colors through your eyes with your sense of *sight*. You perceive sounds through your ears with your sense of *hearing*. Your eyes and your ears are your most important sense organs.* You can perceive shapes, sizes and sounds with your sense of *touch*, too.

There are other things, however, that you can perceive with your sense of touch that you cannot perceive as easily with your eyes and ears. With your sense of touch you can tell easily whether some-

* See YOUR EYES and YOUR EARS by the same authors, The John Day Company, New York.

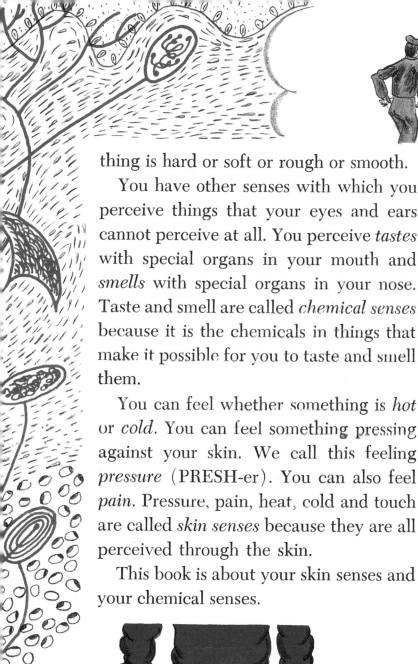

thing is hard or soft or rough or smooth.

You have other senses with which you perceive things that your eyes and ears cannot perceive at all. You perceive *tastes* with special organs in your mouth and *smells* with special organs in your nose. Taste and smell are called *chemical senses* because it is the chemicals in things that make it possible for you to taste and smell them.

You can feel whether something is *hot* or *cold*. You can feel something pressing against your skin. We call this feeling *pressure* (PRESH-er). You can also feel *pain*. Pressure, pain, heat, cold and touch are called *skin senses* because they are all perceived through the skin.

This book is about your skin senses and your chemical senses.

The Electrical Network Inside You

Your body is made up of small parts called *cells* (SELLS). There are many different kinds of cells in your body. There are bone cells and blood cells. There are muscle cells, skin cells and nerve cells. Each kind of cell has its own special job to do. There are some nerve cells whose job it is to make the senses work. They are called *sensory nerve cells.*

Another name for a nerve cell is a *neuron* (NYOU-ron). Every neuron has *nerve endings* which usually look like the branches of a tree and a *nerve fiber* or *axon* (AX-on) which is like a thin thread. The axons of many neurons are covered with a fatty material called *myelin* (MY-uh-lin).

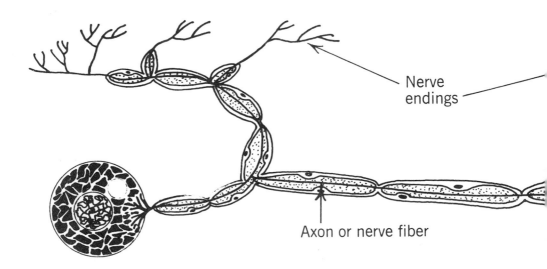

Nerve endings

Axon or nerve fiber

Anything that makes a nerve cell get to work is called a *stimulus* (STIM-yuh-lus). The smallest stimulus that makes a nerve cell get to work is called its *threshold* (THRESH-old). When a neuron is *stimulated* (STIM-yuh-late-ed) it begins to produce little spurts or *impulses* (IM-pul-ses) of electricity. The electrical impulses produced by a neuron travel through its axon to the nerve endings of another neuron. This is how electrical impulses travel from one part of the body to another. So the neurons are like an electrical network inside you.

Electrical impulses produced by neurons may travel as fast as 325 feet in a second or as slowly as 4 feet in a second. The "fast" neurons usually have large axons covered with myelin. The "slow" neurons usually have very fine axons that have no myelin covering.

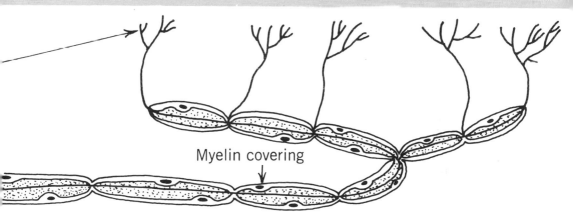

Myelin covering

A sensory nerve cell or neuron

Messages to the Brain

Some sensory nerve cells end in the nose. Some sensory nerve cells end in the mouth. Some end in the eyes, some in the ears and some in the skin. The nerve endings of sensory nerve cells are called *receptors* (ree-SEP-turs) because they receive *stimuli* (STIM-yuh-lie — more than one stimulus are stimuli).

When light strikes your eye, it stimulates the receptors in your eye to produce electrical impulses. The impulses are passed on from the sensory nerve cells in which they were produced to other neurons which carry them to your brain. Your brain is made up of thousands of millions of nerve cells. When electrical impulses from your eye reach your brain, your brain understands them

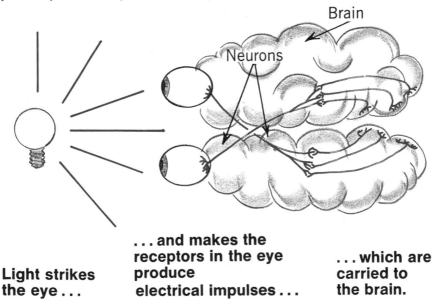

Brain

Neurons

Light strikes
the eye . . .

. . . and makes the
receptors in the eye
produce
electrical impulses . . .

. . . which are
carried to
the brain.

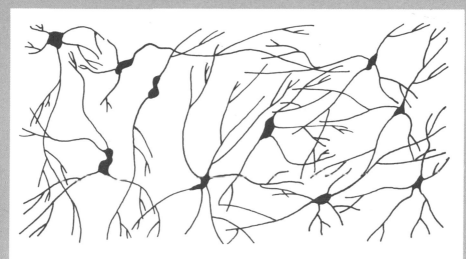

A network of nerve cells in the brain

as light. In the same way, when a smell reaches your nose, it stimulates the smell receptors in your nose to send electrical impulses to your brain. Your brain understands these impulses as a smell or *odor*.

Each receptor can work only in its own special way. The receptors in your eye usually send impulses to your brain only when they have been stimulated by light. However, banging your eye very hard can also stimulate the receptors in your eye to produce electrical impulses. But the only way your brain can understand these impulses is as light. So a hard blow on your eye makes you see flashes of light. We call this "seeing stars." For the same reason, an electric shock on your tongue will produce a sensation of taste and a hard blow on your ear will make your ear "ring."

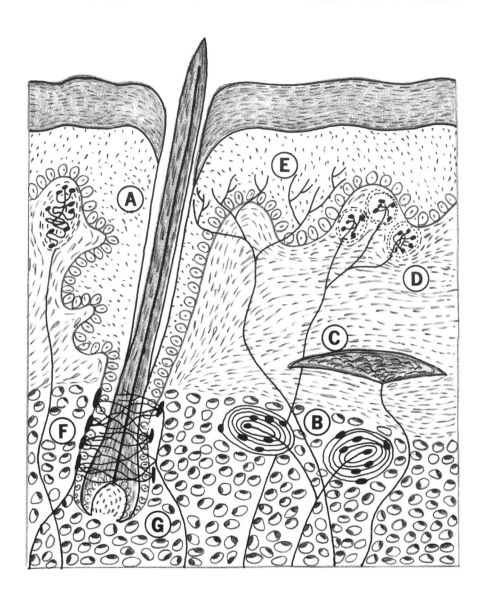

The Skin Senses

The picture on this page is of a slice of skin as it would look under a microscope. The picture shows some of the different skin sense receptors and where they are located.

10

Each skin sense receptor has its own special shape. The skin sense receptors for heat, cold and pressure and some of the touch receptors are in little *structures* (STRUCK-churs) shaped like capsules. These receptors have been named for the scientists who discovered them. The chart on this page gives their names. Pain receptors look like the branches of a tree. In the picture there are pain receptors near the surface of the skin (E) and around the root of the hair (F). There are touch receptors around the root of the hair, too (G).

From the picture you can see that the skin is not covered all over with receptors. There are spaces between the receptors. There are about 200 thousand receptors for hot and cold sensations. There are about half a million receptors for touch and pressure. There are about 3 million receptors for pain. Can you think of a reason why it is useful to have so many pain receptors?

Capsule-shaped receptors

Receptor	Skin Sense	Name of Receptor
A	Touch	Meissner's corpuscle (MICE-nurz KAWR-puh-suhl)
B	Pressure	Pacinian (puh-SIN-ee-un) corpuscle
C	Heat	Ruffini's (roo-FEE-neez) end organ
D	Cold	Krause's (KROUZE-uz) end bulb

A blind person reads Braille with his sense of touch.

Touch

If you brush your fingertips lightly over a surface, the sensation you feel is touch. You have felt a sensation of touch because there are touch receptors in your fingertips. In fact, the touch receptors in your fingertips are closer together than anywhere else in your skin. This is very useful for us, because we learn a lot by just handling objects. It is especially useful for blind people who read by running their fingers lightly over a special kind of raised letter called Braille (BRAIL). Touch receptors are closest together in the tip of the tongue. This is very useful for dogs and animals that learn by touching things with their tongues.

The fingertips and the tongue have no hair. So the only touch receptors your fingertips and tongue have are Meissner's corpuscles. On hairy parts of the body there are also touch receptors that spiral around the roots of the hairs. It is because of this fact that you can feel a light touch on your hair even though hair is dead. The fact that hair is sensitive to touch is useful to certain animals. It is especially useful to animals in the cat family. These animals all have whiskers. A cat can perceive an object in the dark when its long, stiff whiskers brush against the object. When the stiff whiskers brush against the object, they begin to *vibrate* (VY-brate) or move back and forth very quickly. In fact, scientists call the whiskers *vibrissae* (vy-BRISS-ee) because they vibrate. When the whiskers vibrate, they stimulate the touch receptors that spiral around them and the cat feels a sensation of touch.

A cat can feel an object in the dark with its long, stiff whiskers.

Experiments with Touch

Here are some touch experiments you can try. The results of some of them will surprise you.

Place a blindfold over your eyes. Have someone touch your skin very lightly with a fine cotton fiber or a fine hair. Can you locate exactly the spot where you were touched? You had no trouble at all finding the spot that was stimulated by touch. However, you could not always do this. It was a skill you learned through many earlier touch experiences.

You may not believe that you had to learn the meaning of touch sensations. So here is another experiment you can try. Rub a pencil back and forth between the tips of two fingers that are next to each other, as in the first picture. How many pencils do you feel? Now rub the pencil between your crossed fingers, as in the second picture. How many pencils do you feel this time? The results will be even more surprising if you close your eyes when you cross your fingers. The first time you felt only one pencil because this is the sensation you are used to when you rub the one pencil between two fingers. The

1 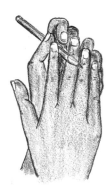   2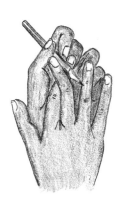

second time you felt two pencils. This happened because, with your fingers crossed, you rubbed the outside of the two fingers at the same time. Your experience has taught you that you can rub the outside of the two fingers at the same time only with two different objects. So you felt two pencils even though you used only one pencil.

Here is another experiment you can try. Take a pair of compasses and separate its two points so that they are about a half inch apart. Now touch the skin of your forearm with the two points at the same time. How many sensations do you feel? You will feel only one touch sensation. Separate the compass points slowly. Keep repeating the experiment until you feel two touch sensations for the first time. Now measure the distance between the two points. It will measure about 1½ inches. Do the same experiment on the tip of your tongue and on your fingertip. Keeping in mind that touch receptors are closest together on the tip of your tongue and on your fingertips, what result do you expect? You can feel two different touch sensations on the tip of your tongue when the compass points are half of a tenth of an inch apart. You can feel two different touch sensations in your fingertips when the compass points are a tenth of an inch apart. On your back, however, you can feel two different sensations only when the compass points are at least 2½ inches apart!

Every part of your body has a *two-point threshold*. It is the smallest distance between the two compass points at which you can feel two touch sensations. In the chart on this page the two-point threshold for each part of the body is shown as the length of a red line.

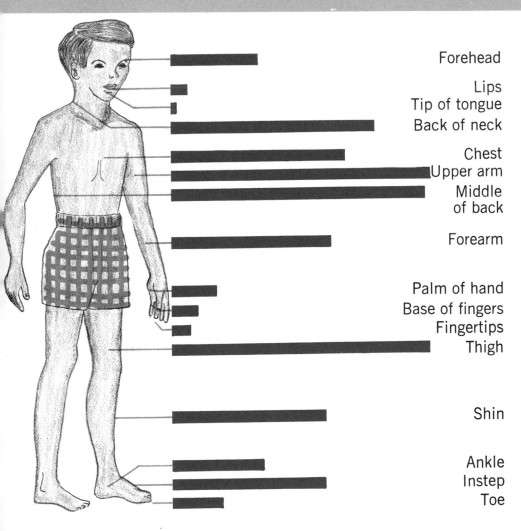

Forehead

Lips
Tip of tongue
Back of neck

Chest
Upper arm
Middle
of back

Forearm

Palm of hand
Base of fingers
Fingertips
Thigh

Shin

Ankle
Instep
Toe

Pressure

If you bring a matchstick toward your arm so that it just touches you, you will stimulate a Meissner corpuscle, the receptor for light touch, and you will feel a touch sensation. As you begin to press down on the match, you will begin to stimulate a Pacinian corpuscle. You will begin to feel a pressure sensation. If you look back at the picture on page 8 you will see why you have to press down on the matchstick to stimulate a pressure receptor. Pressure receptors are not as near the surface of the skin as touch receptors are.

Pressure receptors do many important jobs for you. They let you know when your clothing is too tight. By warning you, they keep you from getting wedged into narrow places. They also help you make judgments about weights.

If you want to find out which of two weights is the heavier, you may lift first one weight and then the other weight. The heavier weight pulls harder on your arms, stimulating more pressure receptors. When more pressure receptors are stimulated, more electrical impulses are sent to your brain. Your brain, in turn, understands this to mean that the weight is heavier.

You cannot always tell, however, which of two weights is the heavier. You cannot tell that a 31-ounce weight is heavier than a 30-ounce weight. But you can tell easily that a 4-ounce weight is heavier than a 3-ounce weight. And you can tell easily that a 40-ounce weight is heavier than a 30-ounce weight. This shows that you cannot always notice a difference between two weights. The smallest *difference that you can just notice* depends on how big the two weights are to begin with. The smallest difference that you can just notice between two heavy weights is bigger than the smallest difference you can just notice between two light weights. This fact was first discovered about 125 years ago by the German scientist, Ernst Weber (VAY-bur).

You can tell easily that a 4-ounce weight is heavier than a 3-ounce weight.

3-ounce
weight

4-ounce
weight

30-ounce
weight

31-ounce
weight

You cannot tell that a 31-ounce weight is heavier than a 30-ounce weight.

But you can tell easily that a 40-ounce weight is heavier than a 30-ounce weight.

30-ounce
weight

40-ounce
weight

Hot and Cold

You can tell the difference easily between something that feels hot and something that feels cold. But sometimes the heat and cold receptors in your skin can fool you. To see how they can, try this experiment.

Fill three basins with water. Fill one with hot water, one with cold water and the third with warm water. Put your right hand in the hot water and your left hand in the cold water. Keep them there a few minutes. Now put both your hands in the warm water. You will find that the warm water will feel cool to your right hand and warm to your left hand.

Your hands felt different temperature sensations because of the way heat behaves. If something hot touches something cold, heat begins to flow from the hot object to the cold object. In the experiment, when you put your right hand in the hot water, the hot water was warmer than your hand. So heat began to flow from the hot water into your hand. This made your right hand hot. As your hand became hot, heat receptors (Ruffini's end organs) in your right hand began to be stimulated. This made your right hand *feel* hot. When you put your left hand in the cold water, your hand was warmer than the water. So heat began to flow from your hand into the cold water. This made your left hand cold. As your hand became colder, cold receptors (Krause's end bulbs) in your left hand began to be stimulated. This made your left hand *feel* cold. Then when you put both hands into the warm water, your right hand was warmer than the water and your left hand was cooler than the water. So heat began to flow from your right hand into the warm

When you put both hands into the warm water, heat began to flow from your right hand into the warm water. So your right hand felt cool.

water, making your right hand cooler. When your right hand became cooler, cold receptors in your right hand began to be stimulated. This made your right hand *feel* cool. At the same time, heat began to flow from the warm water into your cold left hand, making your left hand warmer. When your left hand became warmer, heat receptors in your left hand began to be stimulated. This made your left hand *feel* warm. So your two hands had different temperature sensations.

Sometimes you can have a sensation of hot and cold at the same time. If you put your hand into very, very hot water, your hot hand will have a sensation of hot and cold at the same time. This happens because there is so much heat in the very, very hot water that it stimulates some cold receptors, too. But when a cold receptor is stimulated, the brain understands it as a cold sensation. So your hand feels hot and cold at the same time. For the same reason, on a very cold day your cold hands will have a sensation of cold and hot at the same time.

At the same time, heat began to flow from the warm water into your cold left hand. So your left hand felt warm.

Pain

It is pleasant to sit in front of a hot campfire on a cool summer night. Sensations of cold, pressure and touch can also be very pleasant. It is unpleasant if a spark from the campfire lands on your bare skin. It is unpleasant because it hurts. It hurts because the spark has stimulated pain receptors in your skin. Pain is never pleasant. We usually try to avoid it.

The feeling of pain is one of your body's protections against injury. If you touch a hot radiator by accident, the pain makes you quickly pull your hand away without even thinking. In this way you protect your hand from being burned badly. If a cut isn't healing properly, it

If you touch a hot radiator by accident . . .   **. . . you quickly pull your hand away.**

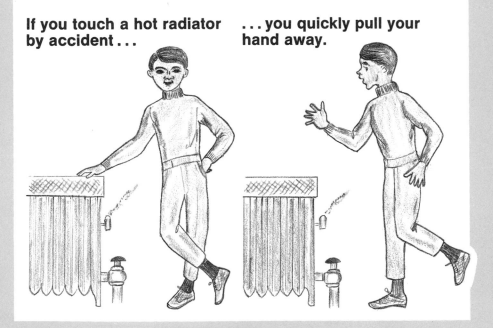

The feeling of pain is one of your body's protections against injury.

hurts a great deal. This is a warning that you ought to have a doctor look after it. A toothache is a warning that your tooth needs the attention of a dentist. A stomachache is a warning that you may have eaten too much food that is not good for your body. Or it may mean something more serious is the matter that needs the attention of a doctor.

Most pain receptors are in the skin. They spread out in fine branchlike structures. Because the pain receptors branch out under the surface of the skin and because there are so many pain receptors, you can perceive pain almost anywhere on the skin. Because most pain receptors are in the skin, surface cuts, scratches, bruises and scrapes hurt more than deeper wounds. There are very few pain receptors in your inner body organs. The liver, the brain and the kidneys can be cut, squeezed or burned without causing any pain. Pain from deep body organs is often not felt as a pain coming from inside but as a pain on the surface of the body. This is called *referred pain.* For example, sores inside the stomach sometimes produce earaches!

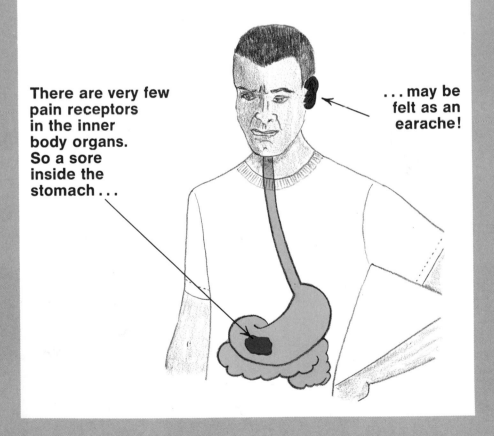

There are very few pain receptors in the inner body organs. So a sore inside the stomach . . .

. . . may be felt as an earache!

Pain receptors send their messages to the brain through two different kinds of nerves. "Fast pain" travels through thick myelin-covered fibers at the speed of 325 feet per second (which is about 220 miles per hour). Fast pain feels sharp, bright or pricking. "Slow pain" travels to the brain about as fast as you can walk. Slow pain has a burning or throbbing sensation. That is why, when you cut your finger, you first feel a sharp pain and then you feel a throbbing pain.

Most people have the same pain threshold. Pain thresholds have been measured by touching the skin with something hot. At first heat receptors are stimulated and only a sensation of heat is perceived. When the heat stimulus is strong enough to make the skin turn red, a sensation of pain is perceived. At this point, the pain threshold has been reached. The amount of heat that was applied to be just perceived as pain is just less than the amount of heat that will damage the cells.

Even though pain thresholds are the same for most people, some people can stand pain better than others. How well you can stand pain depends on your attitude. Certain Indian tribes considered an Indian brave if he held a burning coal in his armpit. So an Indian who wanted to prove that he was brave could stand the pain of burning coals. Soldiers who have received serious

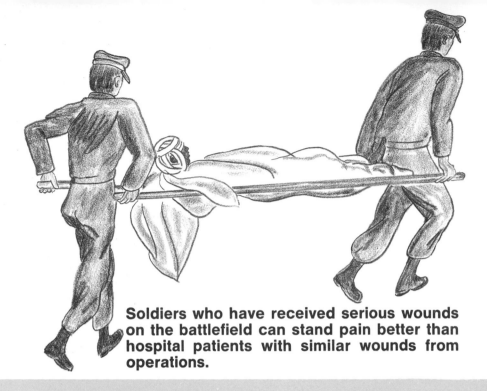

Soldiers who have received serious wounds on the battlefield can stand pain better than hospital patients with similar wounds from operations.

wounds on the battlefield can stand the pain better than hospital patients with similar wounds from operations. The soldier's attitude is one of thankfulness that he has escaped from the battlefield alive. The patient's attitude is often that he is afraid that he may die. So it is *fear of pain* that often makes people unable to stand it.

There are some people who do not have normal thresholds to pain. There are some people who can feel almost no pain at all. Like people who are colorblind, these people are born this way. As children, they injure themselves again and again, because they lack a normal pain warning system. After many injuries, they finally learn how to avoid situations that may cause injury.

26

There are some people who feel pain even when there is no stimulus to produce it. Most people who have had fingers, toes, arms or legs cut off or *amputated* (AM-pyuh-TATE-ed) report that they can still feel the limb that isn't there. They can feel a *phantom* (FAN-tum) or imaginary limb. Some of these people report that the phantom limb hurts. Doctors call this *phantom limb pain.* Sometimes the pain lasts for a long time. No one knows what causes it.

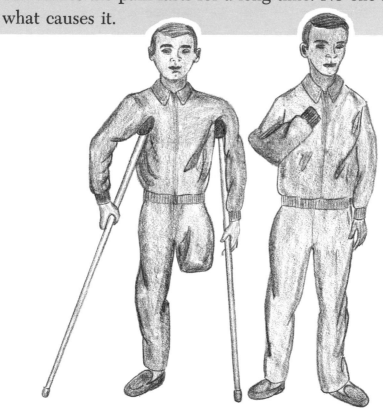

Most people who have had arms or legs amputated report that they can still feel the limb that isn't here.

When you go swimming, at first the water feels cold. After a while, your body gets used to the feeling of cold.

Getting Used to Sensations

When you go swimming, at first the water feels cold. After you have been in the water for a while, it doesn't feel cold any more. Your body has become used to the feeling of cold. When you put your clothes on in the morning, at first you notice the sensation your clothing produces on your skin. It is a sensation of pressure and touch at the same time. After a while you don't notice this sensation any more. Your body has become used to the feeling of being dressed.

Your body can get used to sensations of heat, cold, pressure and touch. It is a good thing that it can, because otherwise you would keep noticing all the stimuli around you. You would be so busy noticing all these stimuli that you would not be able to pay attention to the important stimuli that help you learn.

Your body can get used to sensations of heat, cold, pressure and touch if the stimuli that produce the sensations do not change. A steady pressure stops stimulating the pressure receptors and your body gets used to the pressure sensation. Your body can continue to feel a pressure sensation only when the pressure stimulus changes fast enough. In the same way, you can continue to feel a sensation of heat, cold and touch only when the heat, cold and touch stimuli change fast enough.

Your body usually does not get used to sensations of pain. Even though pain is unpleasant, it is a good thing that this is so. Otherwise, the built-in system that warns your body of injury or danger would not do its job very well.

Pain-killers

We can sometimes get rid of pain by getting rid of the stimulus that produces pain. For example, if you hurt your bare foot by stepping on a pebble, you get rid of the pain by lifting your foot.

Sometimes we cannot get rid of a stimulus that produces pain. If a pain is caused by an incurable illness, the illness is the stimulus and we cannot get rid of it. If a pain is caused by a doctor's scalpel when he performs an operation, the cut of the scalpel is the stimulus and we cannot get rid of it. In these cases the pain is so great that the body cannot stand it. Then it is necessary to get rid of the pain without getting rid of the stimulus. We do this by using a "pain-killer."

Aspirin is an example of a pain-killer. It deadens pain but does not affect other sensations. Pain-killers, such as aspirin, are called *analgesics* (AN-uhl-JEE-ziks).

Pain-killers that deaden all sensations are called *anesthetics* (AN-iss-THED-diks). Anesthetics like *novocaine* (NO-vuh-cane) are sometimes used by dentists when they drill or pull out teeth. The novocaine is injected into the gum, near the tooth to be treated. For about an hour after the injection the gum and the tooth can feel no pain. They feel no other skin sensations either. Your gum feels *numb*. It feels the way your foot feels when it falls asleep. The anesthetic effect of novocaine is *local*.

30

It affects only the area near the injection. Novocaine is an example of a *local anesthetic*.

When a surgeon performs a serious operation, it is usually best if the patient is not aware of what is happening. Then a *general anesthetic* is used. The effect of a general anesthetic is very much like sleep. A general anesthetic may be injected into the bloodstream of the patient. Or it may be breathed in through a mask.

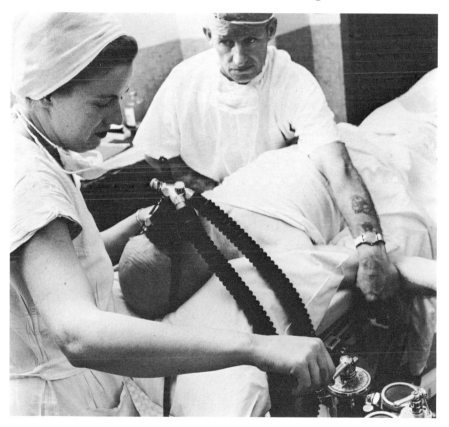

A general anesthetic being breathed in through a mask

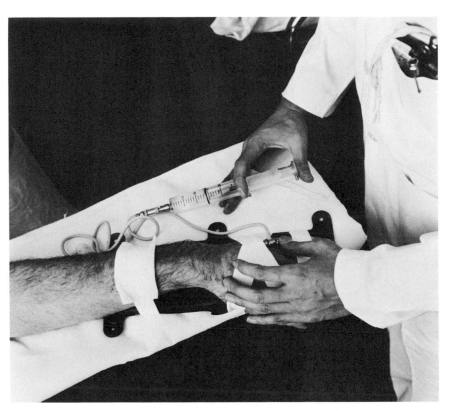

A general anesthetic being injected into the bloodstream

Scientists do not know exactly how anesthetics work. They think that anesthetics may affect the myelin coverings of nerve fibers and interfere with the way the nerve fibers pass on electrical impulses. They feel that the most important effect of anesthetics is on the patient's mind. They have the effect of getting rid of fear. Since fear of pain is one of the reasons why we feel pain, getting rid of the fear helps get rid of pain.

Anesthetics and Surgery

Hundreds of years ago the Indians of Peru used the leaves of the coca plant to help get rid of pain. They would chew on the coca leaves and then spit the chewed-up leaves on a painful wound. The chemical in the coca plant that relieved pain was *cocaine* (KO-kane). Cocaine was one of the first local anesthetics ever used. It was first used in 1884.

More than 100 years before cocaine was used, *nitrous oxide* (NY-trus OX-ide) was discovered by Joseph Priestley. Priestley was the English minister-scientist who discovered oxygen. Priestley did not suspect that nitrous oxide could be used as an anesthetic. Twenty-five years later, Humphry Davy, another English scientist, discovered that nitrous oxide could cure headaches. Nobody paid any attention to his discovery at the time. Nitrous

Many Indians of South America who do not have enough to eat chew cocoa leaves to get rid of hunger pains. This Indian woman is selling dried cocoa leaves.

oxide was not used as an anesthetic until 1844. It was used in a tooth extraction. Nitrous oxide is commonly called "laughing gas" because it produces a feeling of happiness and even produces laughter in the person to whom it is given.

The use of a general anesthetic for surgery did not become popular until after 1846. In October of that year, William T. G. Morton, a Massachusetts dentist and surgeon, demonstrated the use of *ether* (E-thur) in an operation, in a Boston hospital. After Morton's demonstration, the number of surgical operations increased. Until anesthetics were used in surgery, operations had to be per-

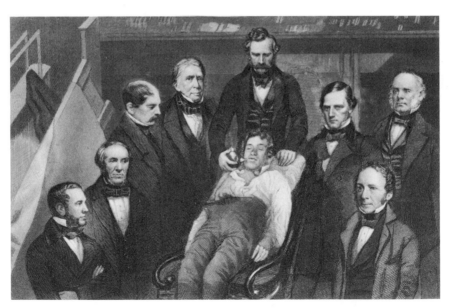

A drawing of William T. G. Morton demonstrating the use of ether in an operation.

formed very quickly because of the great pain the patient had to bear. When operations had to be performed quickly, a surgeon couldn't spend much time worrying about cleanliness and germs. But germs caused infections and many patients died. So operations weren't very popular. When anesthetics were used, a surgeon could take more time during an operation. Only then did surgeons begin to pay attention to the idea that germs caused infections. Only then did they begin to sterilize everything that was used in an operation. Sterilization prevents infections and saves many lives. Since the time of Morton, ether and chemicals related to ether have been used a great deal as general anesthetics.

An Austrian surgeon used cocaine as a local anesthetic in surgery for the first time. But cocaine couldn't be used on everyone. It poisoned some people. Besides, cocaine couldn't be made free of germs. So scientists set to work to see if they could make an anesthetic that didn't have these problems. In 1904 they succeeded in making novocaine. Novocaine works very much the way cocaine does as an anesthetic. It has no harmful effects, however. Novocaine is used a lot as a local anesthetic by dentists and doctors.

Scientists continue to search for new ways of relieving pain that will be safer and better than the anesthetics that have been discovered so far.

Animal Taste and Smell

The taste of good food and the smell of sweet flowers are pleasant sensations. But we usually don't think of our sense of taste and our sense of smell as important senses. This is because we learn so much with our eyes and ears that we do not depend very much on taste and smell.

Although taste and smell are not the most important senses for man, they are very important senses for many animals.

Most animals select the food they eat because of the way it tastes and smells. Using taste and smell as their guide, they select the food that is best for them. Bees are attracted to flowers because of their sweet smell. *Nectar* (NECK-tur), the sweet liquid made by these flowers, is the bee's food. Moths and butterflies have taste receptors in their feet. When a moth or butterfly lands on the sweet part of a flower, the taste receptors in its feet are stimulated. This makes it uncoil its long tongue and sip up the flower's nectar.

Many animals use their sense of smell to find a mate. A male silkworm moth can detect a female moth three miles away by her smell.

Many animals depend on their sense of smell to warn them of danger. A deer can detect the smell of the hunter; a mouse can detect the smell of a cat.

Some saltwater fish depend on their sense of smell to help them locate the freshwater streams where they lay their eggs. Using its sense of smell the salmon travels thousands of miles back to its home stream to *spawn*.

Tastes and smells are useful to certain animals and plants as protections. The bad odor produced by a skunk keeps enemies away. The bitter taste of the Monarch butterfly keeps birds from eating it.

Deer run to safety after detecting the smell of a hunter.

Man's Sense of Smell

Your eyes, ears and skin senses are stimulated by the *physical properties* of things. Light, sound, temperature and pressure are all physical properties.

Smell and taste are stimulated by the *chemical properties* of things. They are stimulated by the *molecules* (MOLL-uh-kyules) in the things you taste and smell. A molecule is the smallest bit of a pure chemical.

You use your nose for smelling. The smell receptors are all located in a small yellow patch of cells high up on the inside of the nose. This area is called the *olfactory* (oll-FAK-tree) area.

For something to be smelled, it must touch the olfactory area. It can do this only if it is carried into the nose by the air you breathe. So something can be smelled if it is a gas that is mixed with the air you breathe.

The air you breathe in follows the path shown by the arrows in the picture. Molecules that produce a smell are carried upward to the olfactory area by small currents of air. When the molecules touch the olfactory area, they stimulate the olfactory receptors. The picture shows what the olfactory receptors look like. The nerve fibers of olfactory cells pass through tiny openings in the base of the skull and end in the brain. The part of the brain where they end is called the *olfactory bulb*. The olfactory bulb is the part of the brain that has to do with smelling.

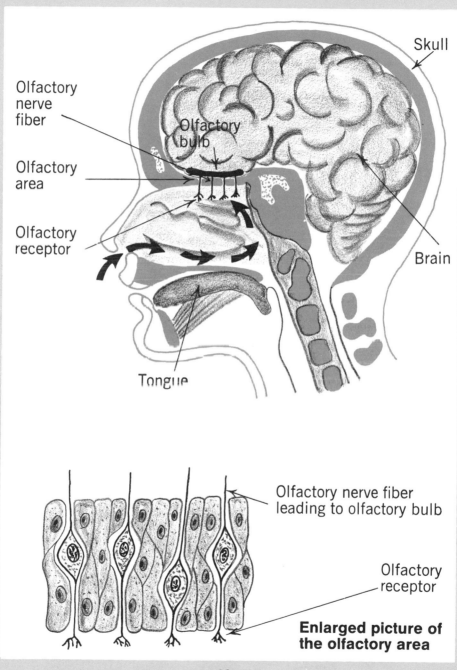

Skull

Olfactory
nerve
fiber

Olfactory
bulb

Olfactory
area

Olfactory
receptor

Brain

Tongue

Olfactory nerve fiber
leading to olfactory bulb

Olfactory
receptor

**Enlarged picture of
the olfactory area**

Facts and Theories About Smell

The sense of smell, like the sense of sight and the sense of hearing, is a *distance sense.* You can detect smells that are produced at a distance from you. You can detect the odor of a skunk that is hundreds of feet away. Unlike sight and hearing, smell is not a *directional sense.* Usually you have no difficulty telling the direction from which a light or a sound comes. You can locate the direction from which a smell comes only by trial-and-error hunting.

You can hear, see and smell things at a distance.

You can smell the chemical a skunk produces when there is only one molecule of it in 60 thousand million molecules of air.

For something to be smelled, it must be able to become a gas at ordinary temperatures. This does not mean that everything that becomes a gas easily has a smell. Water becomes a gas easily, but water has no smell.

You can smell even tiny quantities of a substance. You can smell the chemical a skunk produces when there is only one molecule of it in 60 thousand million molecules of air. This is your smell threshold for this chemical. A dog has a lower threshold for skunk ordor. It can smell one molecule of it in 20 million million molecules of air.

Just as you get used to skin sensations, you get used to smells. If a smell doesn't get stronger, you usually stop noticing it. This is good for people who must work where there are unpleasant smells. If the stimulus of a certain smell lasts for a long time, then you may not be able to smell other smells that are like it. For example, the smell of camphor interferes with your smelling cloves and ether.

You can smell something better by sniffing in short quick puffs. Sniffing increases the number of molecules that touch the olfactory area.

When you have a head cold, you can hardly smell anything at all. The cold makes the lining of your nose swell up and you cannot breathe through your nose. So molecules of the chemicals you usually smell cannot reach the olfactory area of your nose. Some people are either partly or entirely smell-blind. They are usually born that way. Smell-blindness is called *anosmia* (uh-NOZ-me-uh).

For a long time scientists have been trying to explain how we smell.

One theory of smell is based on the vibrations of the atoms within the molecules of the things we smell. According to this theory, these vibrations stimulate the olfactory receptors. Chemicals that vibrate in the same way will smell the same.

Another theory of smell is based on the shapes of the molecules of the things we smell. According to this theory, there are seven kinds of odor that we can smell. Most odors are made up of one or more of these kinds. There are seven different kinds of bowl-shaped receptors, one for each kind of odor. To be smelled, a molecule must fit into a particular receptor. All molecules with the same shape will fit into the same kind of receptor. So they all smell the same. For example, all molecules that smell flowery are banjo-shaped and fit into a banjo-shaped receptor.

There are many other theories of smell, too. So far, however, no theory fits all the facts.

Top view of three different kinds of bowl-shaped receptors . . .

. . . and some molecules that fit into them

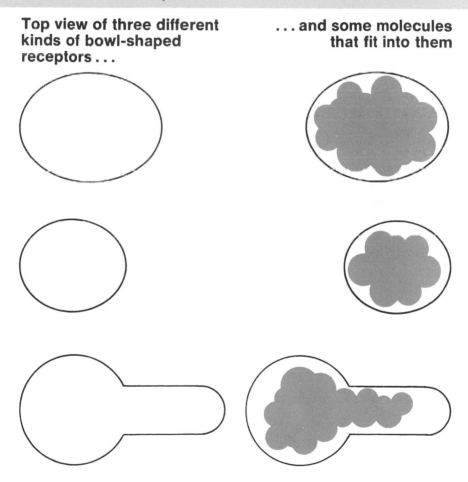

Man's Sense of Taste

Your tongue is the organ with which you taste. The upper surface of your tongue looks velvety. It gets its velvety look from hundreds of little bumps that cover its surface. These bumps are called *papillae* (puh-PILL-ee). The underside of your tongue has no papillae. That is why it looks smooth.

Each *papilla* (puh-PILL-uh) has taste receptors in its surface. The taste receptors are called *taste buds*. There are some taste receptors in your throat, too.

Although you can recognize the tastes of many different foods, your taste buds can perceive only four different tastes. Each taste is perceived by a different part of the tongue. You taste *sweet* things with the tip of your

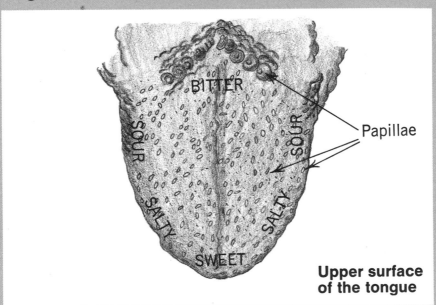

Upper surface of the tongue

tongue. That is why you lick an ice cream cone or a lolli-pop. You taste *bitter* things toward the back of your tongue. That is why you may not notice a bitter taste as quickly as you notice a sweet taste. *Salty* and *sour* tastes are felt along the sides of the tongue.

You can taste something only if it can dissolve in water. Then it can dissolve in the saliva in your mouth, too.

What you usually call the "taste" of food is really the result of several different sensations. The "taste" of a food depends on what it smells like as well as what it really tastes like. Little currents of air carry the food odor up the back of your throat to the olfactory area in your nose. That is why, when you have a cold and your nose is stopped up, food does not taste as good as it usually does. The "taste" of a food also depends on whether it is crisp or soggy or smooth or lumpy. These sensations are felt through touch and pressure receptors in your tongue.

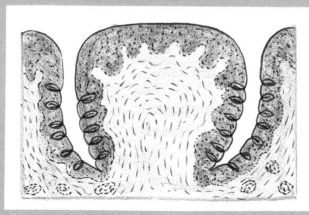

A cutaway picture of a papilla. Taste buds are shown in red.

"Taste" can also depend on the stimulation of heat and cold receptors in your tongue. Something *peppery* stimulates heat receptors. Something *minty* stimulates cold receptors.

Taste thresholds are much higher than smell thresholds. You need much more of a substance to detect it by taste than you do to detect it by smell. Most people have about the same threshold for salt and sugar. You cannot detect salt unless there is one molecule of it in 1500 molecules of water. You cannot detect sugar unless there is one molecule of it in 2500 molecules of water. You can detect *quinine*, which is very bitter, when there is only one molecule of it in 100 million molecules of water.

There are many people who are blind to certain tastes. They are born that way. The chemical *phenyl thiourea* (FEN-uhl thi-o-YOU-re-a — P.T.C. for short) is bitter to some people and tasteless to others. If you can get some P.T.C., taste it to find out if you are a *taster* or a *nontaster*. Another chemical, *benzoate of soda* (BEN-zuh-wait), is tasteless to most people. However, there are some people who find it bitter and others who find it sweet.

Scientists believe that the stimulation of taste receptors probably depends on the size and shape of the molecules in the things we taste. They are still looking for a good theory to explain how we taste.

Word List

Analgesic (AN-uhl-JEE-zik) — A pain-killer that deadens pain but does not affect other sensations.

Anesthetic (AN-iss-THED-dik) — A pain-killer that deadens all sensations.

Axon (AX-on) — The threadlike part of a nerve cell that carries electrical impulses away from the cell to other nerve cells or to the brain.

Cell (SELL) — The smallest living part of your body.

Molecule (MOLL-uh-kyule) — The smallest bit of a pure chemical.

Myelin (MY-uh-lin) — An axon's fatty covering.

Neuron (NYOU-ron) — A nerve cell.

Olfactory (oll-FAK-tree) — Relating to the sense of smell.

Papilla (puh-PILL-uh) — One of the many bumps in the upper surface of the tongue.

Perceive (pur-SEEVE) — To see, hear, taste or smell something.

Receptor (ree-SEP-tur) — The nerve endings of a sensory nerve. They receive stimuli.

Stimulus (STIM-yuh-lus) — Anything that makes a nerve cell get to work.

Taste bud — The receptor for taste.

Threshold (THRESH-old) — The smallest stimulus that makes a nerve cell get to work.

About the Authors

IRVING and RUTH ADLER have written more than sixty books about science and mathematics. Dr. Adler has been an instructor in mathematics at Columbia University and at Bennington College, and was formerly head of the mathematics department of a New York City high school. Mrs. Adler, who formerly taught mathematics, science and art in schools in the New York area, recently also taught at Bennington. In addition to working with her husband writing this book, she has joined with him on 24 other titles in the *Reason Why* series and drawn the illustrations for most of them as well as for many other books written by him.

Books by Irving Adler alone and books by him in collaboration with Ruth Adler have been printed in 83 different foreign editions, in 14 languages and in 10 reprint editions.

The Adlers now live in the country in the Town of Shaftsbury, near Bennington, Vermont.

PICTURE CREDITS

Page 12 — The Lighthouse, The New York
Association for the Blind
Pages 31 and 32 — Paul Weller
Page 34 — Dr. Henry K. Beecher